What do I do
When I Miss You

Janet McMahon

WestBow Press books may be ordered through booksellers or by contacting:

WestBow Press
A Division of Thomas Nelson & Zondervan
1663 Liberty Drive
Bloomington, IN 47403
www.westbowpress.com
844-714-3454

Illustrations by Sundas Gill

ISBN: 978-1-6642-8536-1 (sc)
ISBN: 978-1-6642-8537-8 (e)

Library of Congress Control Number: 2022922335

Print information available on the last page.

WestBow Press rev. date: 01/17/2023

WestBow
PRESS®
A DIVISION OF THOMAS NELSON
& ZONDERVAN

What do I do
When I Miss You

When we are together,
we always have fun.
We play on the swing
and sing silly songs.

We snuggle up to
watch a movie
and have a snack.

We color pictures for
me to take home.

Sometimes it's bath night and I help you get squeaky clean.

When it's time to
go, we hug tight
and wave goodbye.

I miss you. Do you
miss me too?
I have an idea.
Try it and see.

Remember my
hug and I will
remember yours.

Feel deep in your heart how much you are loved.

Think of all the
fun we had.
Think as hard
as you can.

Remember when we were swinging, and singing silly songs? I do. How about you?

Remember watching
our favorite movie
and sharing a snack?
I do. How about you?

Remember the
pictures we colored
for me to take home?
I do. How about you?

Remember the big
towel I wrapped you
up in after your bath?
I do. How about you?

Someone else
who loves you
remembers too.
It's Jesus in Heaven.

You can tell Jesus who you miss.
He likes to hear from you

Tell him how you feel.
If you're happy or sad or
even worried or mad.

He will help you.
His promises are always true.

That's what I do when I miss you.

Printed in the United States
by Baker & Taylor Publisher Services